Asian Animals

Tigers

ABDO
Publishing Company

Big Buddy BOOKS
Asian Animals

by Julie Murray

VISIT US AT
www.abdopublishing.com

Published by ABDO Publishing Company, PO Box 398166, Minneapolis, Minnesota 55439.

Copyright © 2013 by Abdo Consulting Group, Inc. International copyrights reserved in all countries. No part of this book may be reproduced in any form without written permission from the publisher. Big Buddy Books™ is a trademark and logo of ABDO Publishing Company.

Printed in the United States of America, North Mankato, Minnesota.
102012
012013

♻ PRINTED ON RECYCLED PAPER

Coordinating Series Editor: Rochelle Baltzer
Editor: Marcia Zappa
Contributing Editors: Stephanie Hedlund, Sarah Tieck
Graphic Design: Maria Hosley
Cover Photograph: *Shutterstock*: neelsky.
Interior Photographs/Illustrations: *Fotosearch.com*: ©photoncatcher36 (p. 5); *Getty Images*: Reinhard Dirscherl (p. 21), Jonathan Kirn (p. 9), J & C Sohns (p. 15), Harri Tahvanainen (p. 17), Steve Winter (p. 29); *Glow Images*: ARCO/Tuengler, S. (p. 7), Juniors Bildarchiv/Juniors (p. 23), Gerard Lacz/Anka Agency (p. 25), SuperStock (p. 27); *iStockphoto*: ©iStockphoto.com/bjdlzx (p. 9), ©iStockphoto.com/HU-JUN (p. 4), ©iStockphoto.com/ ricardoreitmeyer (p. 19), ©iStockphoto.com/Snowleopard1 (p. 25); *Shutterstock*: Volodymyr Burdiak (pp. 11, 13), jo Crebbin (p. 29), Pichugin Dmitry (p. 8), Fakhri Hilmi (p. 9), Image Focus (p. 4), fuyu liu (p. 8), neelsky (p. 11), Oleinikova Olga (p. 13), Andre Schaerer (p. 19).

Library of Congress Cataloging-in-Publication Data

Murray, Julie, 1969-
 Tigers / Julie Murray.
   p. cm. -- (Asian animals)
 Audience: 7-11
 ISBN 978-1-61783-558-2
 1. Tiger--Asia--Juvenile literature. I. Title.
 QL737.C23M87 2013
 599.756095--dc23
                           2012030917

Contents

Long ago, nearly all land on Earth was one big mass. About 200 million years ago, the land began to break into **continents**. One of these continents is Asia.

Tigers are known for their strength, beauty, and large size.

Asia is the largest **continent**. It includes many countries and **cultures**. It also has different types of land and interesting animals. One of these animals is the tiger. In the wild, tigers are only found in Asia.

Tiger Territory

There are several types of tigers. These include Bengal, Indo-Chinese, Malayan, Siberian, and Sumatran tigers.

Tigers are found in small areas across Asia. They can live in many different **habitats**. They just need shade, water, and food. Tigers live in wet areas, rain forests, and dry woods. Some even live in cold, snowy forests.

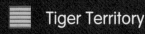 Tiger Territory

Bengal tigers are the most common type of tiger.

Welcome to Asia!

If you took a trip to where tigers live, you might find…

…lots of people.

Tigers avoid people. Yet, they live in two of the world's most-populated countries! China is first, with about 1.3 billion people. India is second, with about 1.2 billion people.

…soaring mountains.

Some tigers live in the Himalayas. This mountain system has the world's highest peak. Mount Everest is more than 29,000 feet (8,800 m) high!

...many countries.

Asia is made up of 50 countries. Many of these have several groups of people within them. These groups each have their own histories and cultures.

...different languages.

Hundreds of languages are spoken across Asia. One common language is Hindi. It uses an alphabet with 44 letters. Another common language is Chinese. Chinese writing (*left*) uses characters instead of letters. Each character represents a word or part of a word.

9

Take a Closer Look

Tigers are the largest members of the cat family. They have thick, powerful bodies. Their large heads have big mouths and noses and small, round ears.

Most adult male tigers are 7 to 13 feet (2 to 4 m) long with their tails stretched out. They weigh 220 to more than 600 pounds (100 to more than 270 kg). Females are smaller than males.

Siberian tigers (*left*) are the largest type of tiger. Sumatran tigers (*above*) are the smallest.

White tigers have all white fur with brown or black stripes. They are common in zoos and shows. But, they are unusual in the wild.

Tigers are known for their striped fur. Most tigers have orange or reddish fur on their backs. They have white fur on their undersides. A tiger's fur is marked by dark gray, brown, or black stripes. No two tigers have the same pattern.

Tigers that live in cold areas have extra long, thick fur.

13

Independent Life

Adult tigers generally live alone. Each one has a home area. Often, a male tiger's home area overlaps with the home areas of several females. This allows them to **mate**

The size of a tiger's home area depends on how much food is available. If food is plentiful, it may be smaller than eight square miles (20 sq km). If food is harder to find, it may be larger than 200 square miles (518 sq km)

Tigers mark their home areas by scratching trees and leaving their scent.

Mighty Hunters

Tigers are carnivores. They mostly eat large animals such as deer, wild pigs, antelope, and water buffalo. Tigers also eat smaller animals including monkeys, birds, and frogs.

Tigers hunt alone. They usually hunt at night. Sometimes, a tiger hides and waits for its prey to come close. Other times, it creeps toward it. When it gets close, it rushes to catch the prey.

Uncovered!
In some parts of Asia, tigers eat young rhinoceroses and elephants.

Hunting is difficult work. Most tigers only catch their prey one in every 10 to 20 tries.

A tiger's stripes help it hide among tall grass and trees.

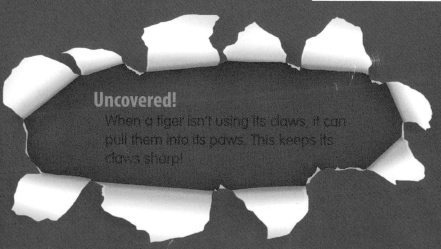

Tigers are well built for hunting. They use their sharp claws and strong front legs to pull down their prey. Or, they use their heavy bodies to knock it down. Then, they use their large, sharp teeth to hold and kill the prey.

Uncovered!
When a tiger isn't using its claws, it can pull them into its paws. This keeps its claws sharp!

Tigers see well in the dark. They also use their sharp hearing to find prey.

Mealtime

After a successful hunt, a tiger drags its catch to a hidden spot. It eats as much as it can. Then, it covers what is left with dirt and leaves.

Later, a tiger will come back to eat more. It can take several days for a tiger to finish eating a large kill.

Uncovered!

A tiger's tongue is rough, like sandpaper. This helps it clean the meat from the bones of its prey.

Tigers can eat more than 40 pounds (18 kg) in one meal! But, they usually eat less.

Baby Tigers

Tigers are **mammals**. Female tigers can have up to seven babies at a time. Most often, they have two or three.

Baby tigers are called cubs. At birth, they weigh two to three pounds (0.9 to 1.4 kg). Newborn tiger cubs are helpless. They count on their mother for care.

A female tiger chooses a hidden spot to give birth and care for her cubs. This may be a cave or a patch of very thick grass.

Newborn tiger cubs are left in a hidden spot while their mother hunts and eats. At first, the cubs drink their mother's milk and grow.

After two to six months, cubs start to follow their mother around. They begin to eat meat from her prey. And, they learn to hunt by watching her. After about two to three years, cubs are ready to live on their own.

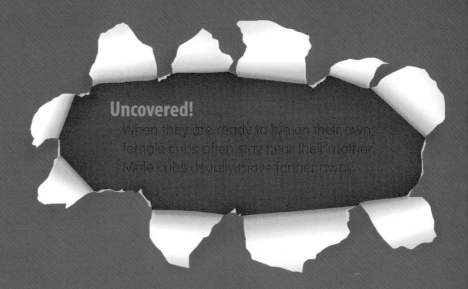

Uncovered!
When they are ready to live on their own, female cubs often stay near their mother. Male cubs usually move farther away.

Tiger cubs grow very quickly.

Cubs are often playful. They chase each other and pretend to fight.

25

Survivors

Life in Asia isn't easy for tigers. Much of their habitat has been lost to logging, buildings, and farms. And, prey is not as common as it once was.

Tigers also risk being killed by people. People hunt them out of fear and to show bravery. They also kill them for their striped fur and to use their body parts in medicine. Today, scientists believe only 3,000 to 5,000 tigers remain in the wild.

Uncovered!

Tigers are feared because they have been known to kill and eat people. But, this is uncommon. Tigers generally attack people only if they can't find or hunt their natural prey. Often, these tigers are sick or hurt.

Tigers are endangered. This means they are in danger of dying out.

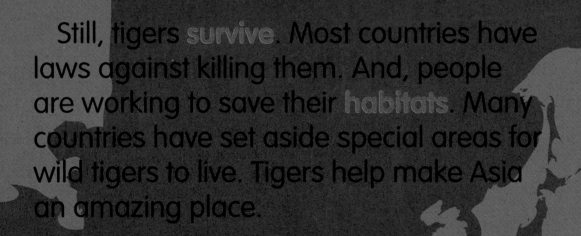

Still, tigers survive. Most countries have laws against killing them. And, people are working to save their habitats. Many countries have set aside special areas for wild tigers to live. Tigers help make Asia an amazing place.

The Hukawng Valley Tiger Reserve in Myanmar is the world's largest area of guarded tiger habitat. It is about the size of the state of Vermont!

In the wild, tigers live for 10 to 20 years.

Uncovered!
In 2010, the leaders of 13 countries home to wild tigers met. They made a plan to double the number of wild tigers by 2022!

Wow!
I'll bet you never knew...

...that tigers and lions have had babies together! Their cubs are called tigons or ligers. These cubs have only been born in zoos and animal parks, not in the wild.

...that tigers are good swimmers. Most types of cats don't like water. But, tigers do! They can swim across rivers and between islands. Tigers can even kill **prey** while swimming.

...that tigers are not picky eaters. If they can't find their usual prey, tigers will hunt other animals. These include sloth bears, dogs, leopards, porcupines, crocodiles, and even pythons.

...that according to the Chinese lunar calendar, 2010 was the Year of the Tiger. This brought a lot of attention to the animal. The next Year of the Tiger will be 2022.

Important Words

carnivore (KAHR-nuh-vawr) an animal or a plant that eats meat.

continent one of Earth's seven main land areas.

culture (KUHL-chuhr) the arts, beliefs, and ways of life of a group of people.

habitat a place where a living thing is naturally found.

mammal a member of a group of living beings. Mammals make milk to feed their babies and usually have hair or fur on their skin.

mate to join as a couple in order to reproduce, or have babies.

medicine (MEH-duh-suhn) an item used in or on the body to treat an illness, ease pain, or heal a wound.

prey an animal hunted or killed by a predator for food.

survive to continue to live or exist.

Web Sites

To learn more about tigers, visit ABDO Publishing Company online. Web sites about tigers are featured on our Book Links page. These links are routinely monitored and updated to provide the most current information available.

www.abdopublishing.com

Index